TH
Sar
Jane
ADVENTURES

BBC CHILDREN'S BOOKS
Published by the Penguin Group
Penguin Books Ltd, 80 Strand, London, WC2R 0RL, England
Penguin Group (USA) Inc., 375 Hudson Street, New York, New York 10014, USA
Penguin Books (Australia) Ltd, 250 Camberwell Road, Camberwell, Victoria 3124, Australia.
(A division of Pearson Australia Group Pty Ltd)
Canada, India, New Zealand, South Africa
Published by BBC Children's Books, 2009

Written by Phil Ford
10 9 8 7 6 5 4 3 2 1

www.thesja.com

ISBN-13: 978-1-40590-629-6
Printed in Great Britain by Clays Ltd, St Ives plc

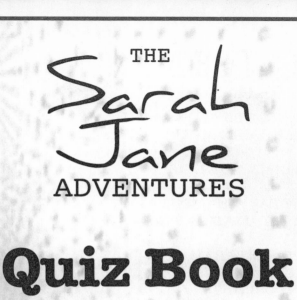

THE Sarah Jane ADVENTURES

Quiz Book

CONTENTS

WHAT DO YOU KNOW ABOUT SARAH JANE SMITH?

Sarah Jane Smith and her loyal gang defend Earth from all kinds of alien threats – but just how much do you really know about her?

1. Where does Sarah Jane live?

   a) Bannerman Road
   b) Flagstaff Road
   c) Bunting Street

2. What is the name of Sarah Jane's alien super-computer?

   a) Mr Jones
   b) Miss Peabody
   c) Mr Smith

3. Where does she keep her computer?

   a) The potting shed
   b) The attic
   c) The cellar

4 What is Sarah Jane's profession?

a) Journalist
b) Private investigator
c) Florist

5 Sarah Jane used to be attached to a military organisation – what was it called?

a) MI6
b) UNIT
c) MJ12

6 Sarah Jane was orphaned as a baby, who brought her up?

a) Aunt Lydia
b) Aunt Laura
c) Aunt Lavinia

7. What is special about Sarah Jane's favourite lipstick?

   a) It won't smudge
   b) It tastes of strawberries
   c) It's sonic

8. Sarah Jane used to go travelling in time and space – with whom?

   a) The Master
   b) The Trickster
   c) The Doctor

9. What really annoys Sarah Jane about her neighbour, Gita Chandra?

   a) She calls her "Sarah" all the time
   b) The way she drives
   c) Her laugh

10. What is special about Sarah Jane's wristwatch?

   a) It can tell you the time on Metebelis 3
   b) It can detect aliens
   c) It can translate any alien language

ANSWERS:

1.a, 2.c, 3.b, 4.a, 5.b, 6.c, 7.c, 8.c, 9.a, 10.b.

THE BANE ARE HERE!

Sarah Jane first met Maria Jackson when she moved into Bannerman Road with her father. The two of them were soon up to their eyes in space creatures in *Invasion of the Bane* – but how much do you remember about that first adventure?

1. What was the name of the villainous Bane leader?

   a) Mrs Windchime
   b) Miss Woodworm
   c) Mrs Wormwood

2. The Bane planned to invade using a soft drink. What was it called?

   a) Bubbleshock
   b) Bubblesgetupyournose
   c) Hubble-bubble

3 What is the name of Maria's new friend who takes her to the Bubbleshock factory?

a) Carrie
b) Kelly
c) Kelsey

4 In what part of the Bane factory did Sarah Jane first meet Luke?

a) The laboratory
b) The ladies' loos
c) The canteen

5 What had to be turned off before tours of the Bubbleshock factory?

a) Cameras
b) Mobile phones
c) Mp3 players

6 When Luke goes to Sarah Jane's house for the first time, how old do we discover he is?

a) 14
b) 360 years
c) 360 minutes

7 When the Bane leader reads the mind of Maria's friend what does she mistakenly believe she worships?

a) The Holy Sycamore
b) The Holy Oak
c) The Holy Spruce

8 What is the name of the Bane who attacks Sarah Jane's house?

a) Donny
b) Danny
c) Davey

9 Before Sarah Jane's final confrontation with the Bane leader, what mode of transport does she use to smash her way into the factory?

a) Her car
b) The TARDIS
c) The Bubbleshock bus

10 What frightening creature lurks in the roof of the Bubbleshock factory?

a) The Bane Mother
b) The Bane Father
c) The Bane Child

ANSWERS: 1.c, 2.a, 3.c, 4.b, 5.b, 6.c, 7.b, 8.c, 9.c, 10.a.

FIRST DAY AT SCHOOL - AND THE HEAD'S AN ALIEN!

In *Revenge of the Slitheen* Maria and Luke start school together, make a new friend – and a world-threatening discovery. See if you can pass this exam...

1. Which planet are the Slitheen from?

   a) Skaro
   b) Metebelis 3
   c) Raxacoricofallapatorius

2. How do the Slitheen disguise themselves as humans?

   a) They are shape-shifters
   b) They wear human skins like a suit of clothes
   c) They use mind control

3. What is the name of Park Vale's headmaster, who turns out to be Slitheen?

   a) Mr Bateman
   b) Mr Baker
   c) Mr Blakeman

4. According to the Slitheen leader, what do humans smell like?

   a) Flowery
   b) Soupy
   c) Horrible

5. What connects all the schools involved in the Slitheen plot?

   a) They are all at the end of tube lines
   b) They all face north
   c) They all have duck ponds

6 What is the first clue that something is wrong at the school?

a) Strange lights in the sky
b) Food going off in the canteen
c) School kids disappearing

7 What does Sarah Jane realise is deadly to the Slitheen?

a) Vinegar
b) Salt water
c) Lemonade

8 What is the name of the company that built the mysterious new science block at Park Vale?

a) Coldfire Construction
b) Coalfire Construction
c) Blob the Builders

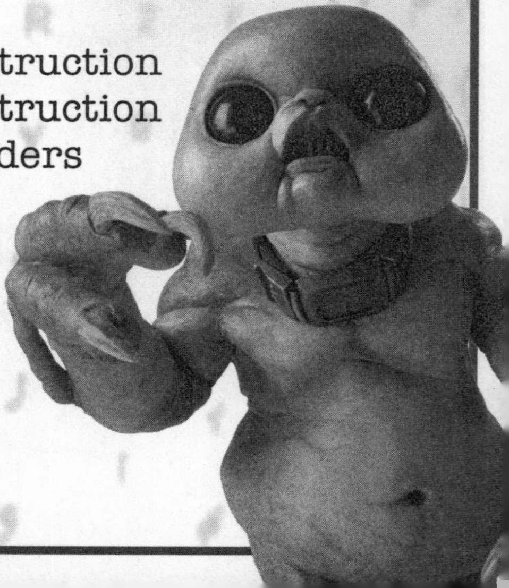

9 Luke tells Sarah Jane he's made a really bad social mistake – what was it?

a) Burping during a lesson
b) Visiting the girls' toilets by mistake
c) Telling the Slitheen how to destroy the world

10 What is the name of the boy who helps Maria and Clyde escape the Slitheen – only to reveal himself as one of them?

a) Colin
b) Craig
c) Carl

ANSWERS: 1.c, 2.b, 3.c, 4.b, 5.a, 6.b, 7.a, 8.a, 9.c, 10.c.

WHAT'S IN SARAH JANE'S ATTIC?

Okay, so we all know that the nerve centre of Sarah Jane's world-saving operations sits at the top of the stairs at 13 Bannerman Road – and that's where you'll find Mr Smith, fanfare and all – but have you really been keeping your eyes open up there?

1. Mr Smith, Sarah Jane's computer, is kept hidden in the chimney.

   TRUE / FALSE

2. Sarah Jane keeps a very small alien galaxy in a jam jar in her safe.

   TRUE / FALSE

3. Sarah Jane keeps a telescope in the attic.

   TRUE / FALSE

4. Sarah Jane has another computer in the attic as well as Mr Smith.

   TRUE / FALSE

5 There is a map of the solar system on the back of the door into the attic.

TRUE / FALSE

6 The couch in Sarah Jane's attic is green.

TRUE / FALSE

7 There is a hat stand beside the door.

TRUE / FALSE

8 There are two other doors leading from the attic.

TRUE / FALSE

9 There are pictures on the walls of the TARDIS.

TRUE / FALSE

10 The newspaper front page pinned to Mr Smith before he opens up is from The Ealing Echo.

TRUE / FALSE

ANSWERS: True. 2. False. 3. True. 4. True. 5. False. 6. False. 7. False. 8. True. 9. True. 10. False.

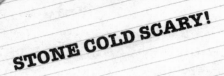

STONE COLD SCARY!

Stories of a haunting catch Sarah Jane's attention and lead her to a confrontation with sinister nuns and a creature from ancient mythology in *Eye of the Gorgon* – try and answer the questions before you get turned to stone!

1. What is the name of the rest home said to be haunted by a nun?

   a) Pearly Gates
   b) Lavender Lawns
   c) Heavenly Hedges

2. What are the sinister nuns searching for?

   a) A key
   b) A jewel
   c) A talisman

3 Bea Nelson-Stanley mentions that she has encountered old enemies of Sarah Jane's – who were they?

a) The Daleks
b) The Cybermen
c) The Sontarans

4 What is the name of the nuns' leader?

a) Sister Helena
b) Sister Carmella
c) Sister Suzie

5 Bea has a secret that she shows Luke. Where is it hidden?

a) Under her bed
b) Inside a clock
c) In a tree

6 What is the name of the rest home manager who is serving the nuns?

a) Mrs Griffiths
b) Mrs Gribbins
c) Mrs Gittings

7 Chrissie comes back to live with Maria and Alan. Why?

a) She finds a spider in her bath
b) She finds an alien in her bath
c) She falls out with her boyfriend, Ivan

8 What sort of car do the nuns drive?

a) Hearse
b) White Rolls Royce
c) Mini Cooper

9. How long does Maria have to prevent her dad from being turned permanently to stone?

a) 90 minutes
b) 60 minutes
c) 30 minutes

10. What does Bea give Maria to help her defeat the gorgon?

a) Another pendant
b) A mirror
c) A hair brush

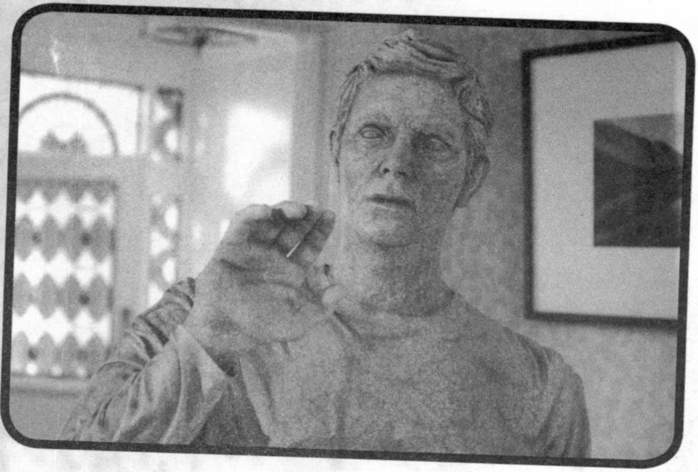

ANSWERS: 1. b, 2. c, 3. c, 4. a, 5. c, 6. b, 7. c, 8. a, 9. a, 10. b.

GENERAL KUDLAK WANTS YOU FOR A SOLDIER!

In *Warriors of Kudlak*, Sarah Jane and her team encounter an alien who needs children to serve as soldiers in a war in a distant galaxy, but will your memory pass muster?

1. What is the name of the laser tag centre at the heart of General Kudlak's plot?

   a) Battleshot 3000
   b) Combat 3000
   c) Warmaster 3000

2. Sarah Jane is investigating the disappearance of a boy – what was his name?

   a) Lance Metcalf
   b) Robin Munro
   c) Leslie Mitcham

3 The boys called the missing boy 'Corporal' – a bad choice as his father was a soldier killed in service. But who made up the nickname?

a) Luke
b) Clyde
c) Brandon

4 What is the name of the human helping Kudlak lure kids into the laser tag centre?

a) Mr Greenham
b) Mr Grantham
c) Mr Griffin

5 During her investigation, Sarah Jane uses a strange machine to collect entanglement shells from the atmosphere – Mr Smith tells us they are used by planet terraformers to do what?

a) Stimulate rainfall
b) Clear the air of pollutants
c) Feed plant life

6 What race is General Kudlak?

a) Sontaran
b) Malakh
c) Uvodni

7 What does Luke use to hack into the spaceship's computer system?

a) The sonic lipstick
b) Clyde's mobile
c) His fountain pen

8 Mr Smith tells Sarah Jane that twenty-four children have disappeared across the country – and each disappearance has coincided with what?

a) An earth tremor
b) Torrential rain
c) Lights in the sky

9. When Clyde and Luke play the laser tag game what numbers are they wearing?

a) 7 and 8
b) 9 and 10
c) 6 and 7

10. What does not compute for Mistress, Kudlak's computer?

a) Peace
b) War
c) Love

ANSWERS: 1.b, 2.a, 3.a, 4.b, 5.a, 6.c, 7.b, 8.b, 9.a, 10.a.

LET'S HEAR IT FOR THE GIRLS!

Maria Jackson moves in across the road from Sarah Jane and discovers that her new neighbour has an amazing secret. Rani Chandra also has no idea how her life is going to be turned upside down the day she moves into the house that used to be Maria's. But both girls have just what it takes to work alongside Sarah Jane to save the world week after week. Let's see how much you really know about them...

1 Why do Maria and her dad move into Bannerman road?

a) They're on the run from aliens
b) Their old house was flattened by a meteor
c) Her parents have split up

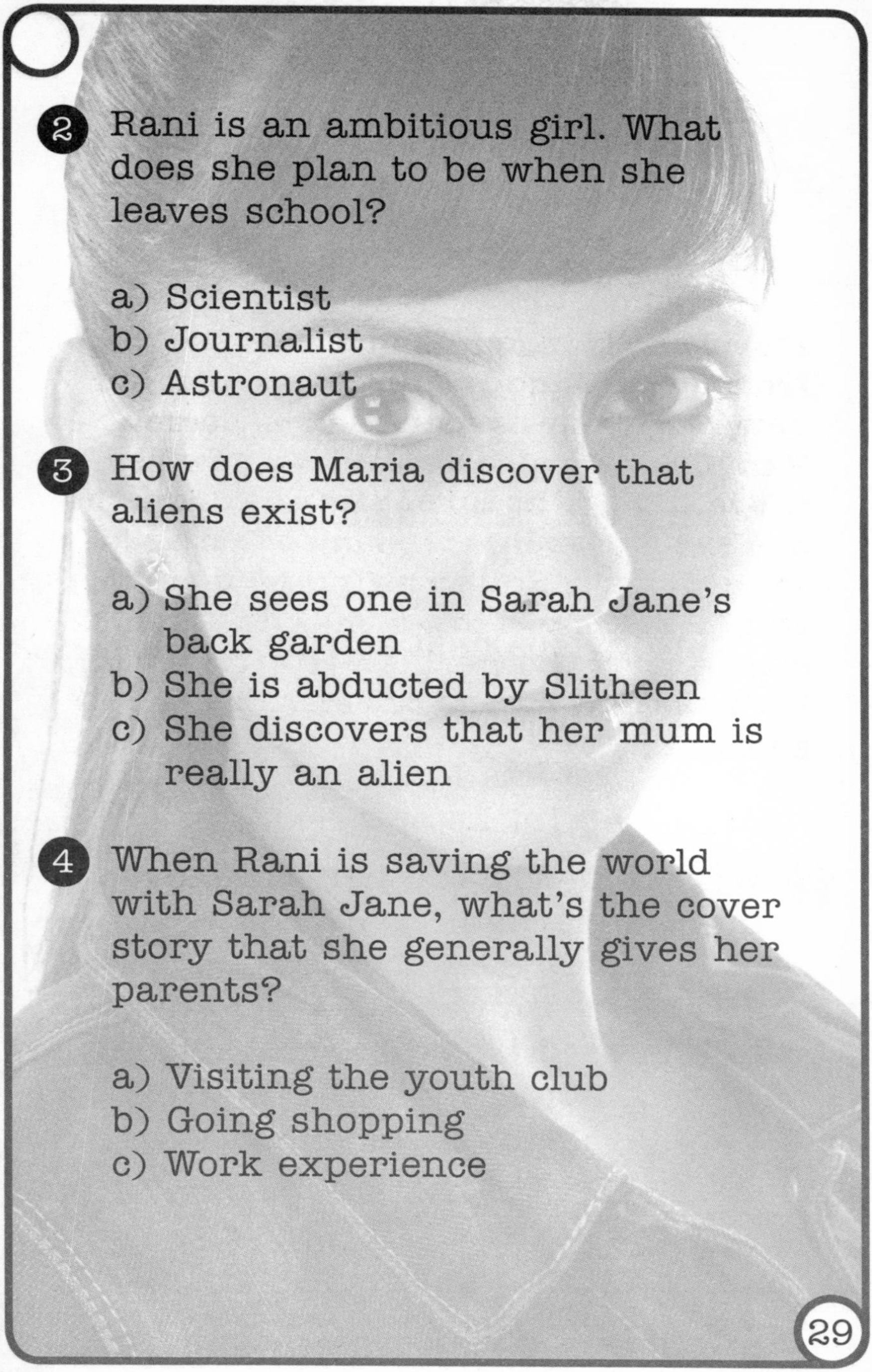

2 Rani is an ambitious girl. What does she plan to be when she leaves school?

a) Scientist
b) Journalist
c) Astronaut

3 How does Maria discover that aliens exist?

a) She sees one in Sarah Jane's back garden
b) She is abducted by Slitheen
c) She discovers that her mum is really an alien

4 When Rani is saving the world with Sarah Jane, what's the cover story that she generally gives her parents?

a) Visiting the youth club
b) Going shopping
c) Work experience

5 Where did Maria first meet Luke?

a) The Bubbleshock factory
b) Sarah Jane's house
c) School

6 What does Sarah Jane give Rani to keep her safe from Odd Bob overnight, which ends up giving Gita a headache?

a) K-9
b) A defence field emitter
c) The sonic lipstick

7 What protects Maria from the Trickster's time warping activities?

a) A puzzle box
b) A jigsaw puzzle
c) A crossword puzzle

8 In what year do we find a very different Rani in Sarah Jane's house during *The Mad Woman in the Attic*?

a) 2059
b) 2020
c) 1940

9 Maria left to live in America – but which city?

a) New York
b) Washington, D.C.
c) Houston

10 When Rani travels back to 1951 to find Sarah Jane she accidentally reveals what?

a) Sarah Jane's true identity
b) That the Trickster is about to destroy the world
c) That Luke has no belly button

ANSWERS: 1.c, 2.b, 3.a, 4.c, 5.a, 6.b, 7.a, 8.a, 9.b, 10.a.

IT'S ANOTHER DAY LIKE ANY OTHER – EXCEPT, WHATEVER HAPPENED TO SARAH JANE?

Maria goes to bed one night and wakes up the next morning to discover a strange woman living in number 13 – there's no Luke, her dad doesn't remember any neighbour called Sarah Jane and Clyde wants to know why Maria has his phone number! It's a very weird and dangerous day – but were you taking notes?

1. What is the name of the meteor hurtling towards Earth?

   a) XL5
   b) K67
   c) Q39

2. What gift does Sarah Jane give Maria in the attic?

   a) A puzzle box
   b) A defence field emitter
   c) A three-dimensional alien chess set

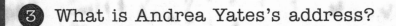

3. What is Andrea Yates's address?

a) 2 Bannerman Road
b) 13 Bannerman Road
c) 8 Bannerman Road

4. Where did the Trickster intervene to change time?

a) Westport Pier
b) Southend Pier
c) Eastend Pier

5. When Maria escapes the Graske, what year does she find herself transported to?

a) 2012
b) 1904
c) 1964

6. What does the Trickster tell Sarah Jane is food to him?

a) Death
b) Chaos
c) Fish and chips

7 7. When the Graske appears at Andrea's party, how does Alan overcome him?

a) He trips him down the stairs
b) He rides his skateboard at him
c) He shoots the Graske with his own weapon

8 8. How old were Andrea and Sarah Jane when the accident happened?

a) 12
b) 10
c) 13

9 9. How does Andrea defeat the Trickster and help save the world?

a) She smashes his reflection in the mirror
b) She smashes the puzzle box
c) She withdraws her agreement

10. When Sarah Jane returns from limbo, how long does she have left to save Earth?

a) 30 seconds
b) 20 seconds
c) 60 seconds

ANSWERS: 1.b, 2.a, 3.b, 4.a, 5.c, 6.b, 7.b, 8.c, 9.c, 10.a.

WHEN COMPUTERS GO BAD

In *The Lost Boy*, just when we think we know who Luke is, Sarah Jane's world is turned upside down by the discovery that his real parents have spent the last few months hunting for him – but are things really as they seem? Can Sarah Jane even trust all her closest allies?

1 Sarah Jane and Luke are waiting in the attic to observe the spectacular Kalazian Lights – but when was the last time this galactic lightshow was visible from Earth?

a) 6,000 years ago
b) 2,000 years ago
c) 4,000 years ago

2 How does Sarah Jane discover that Luke might, in fact, be a missing child called Ashley Stafford?

a) The police contact her
b) She sees a press conference on TV
c) She sees a photograph in the paper

3 Who tips off the police that Sarah Jane has the 'missing' boy living with her?

a) Mrs Wormwood
b) Alan Jackson
c) Chrissie Jackson

4 Ashley Stafford's parents are actually aliens posing as humans – what are they?

a) Slitheen
b) Sontarans
c) Krillitane

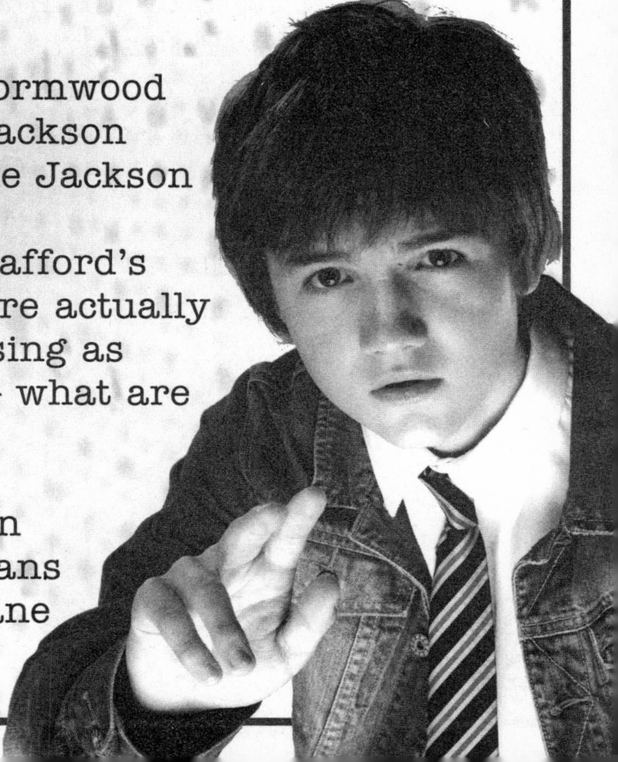

5 The aliens are involved in a plot with Mr Smith – but through which household object do they stay in contact with him?

a) Telephone
b) Televison
c) Radio

6 What is the name of the organisation that Sarah Jane learns has been using alien technology to tap human telekinetic energy?

a) UNIT
b) The Pharos Institute
c) Torchwood

7 What is the name of the obnoxious child genius that Sarah Jane encounters with an IQ greater than Einstein's?

a) Roderick Quiller
b) Jason Fletcher
c) Nathan Goss

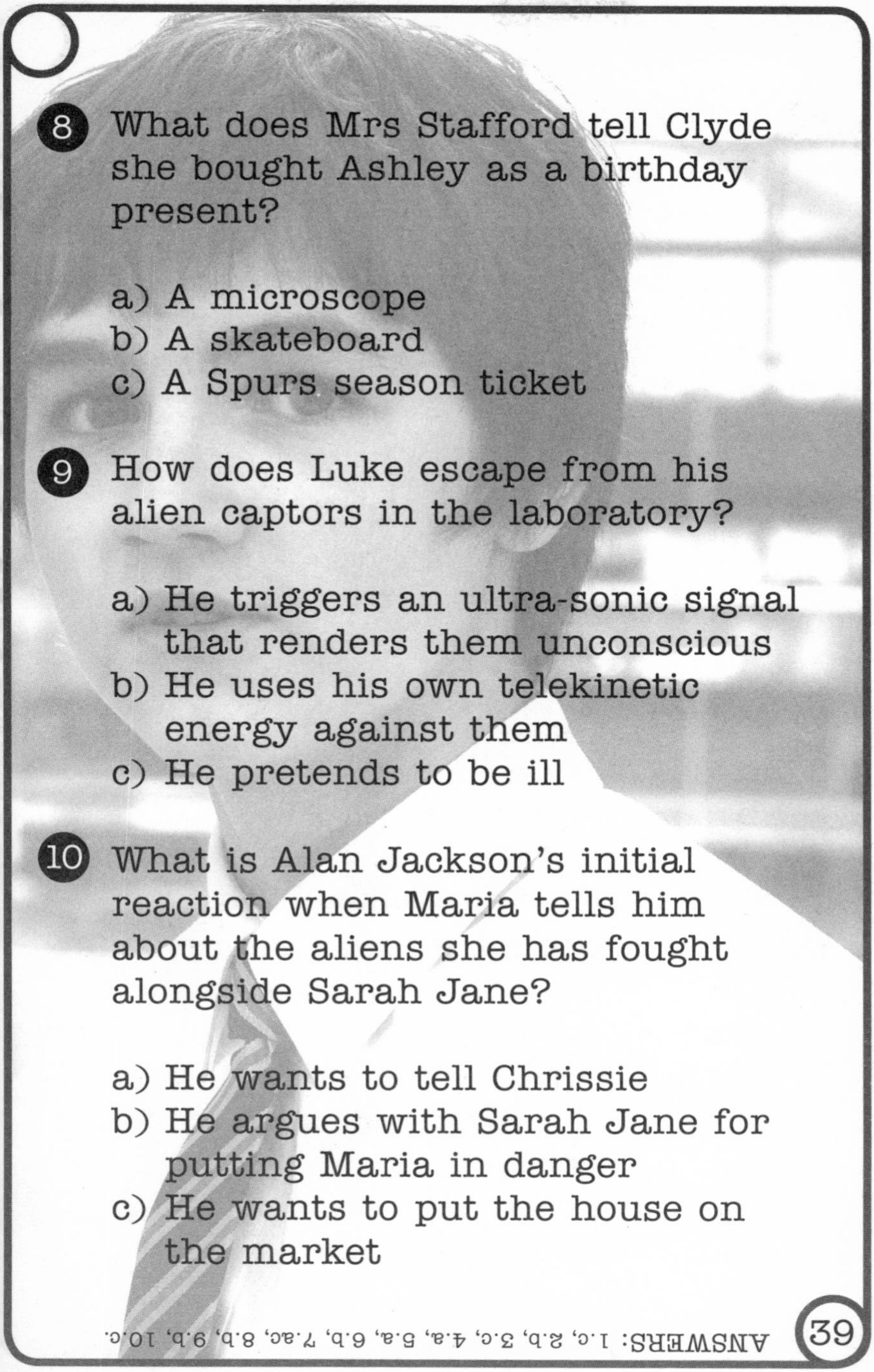

8 What does Mrs Stafford tell Clyde she bought Ashley as a birthday present?

a) A microscope
b) A skateboard
c) A Spurs season ticket

9 How does Luke escape from his alien captors in the laboratory?

a) He triggers an ultra-sonic signal that renders them unconscious
b) He uses his own telekinetic energy against them
c) He pretends to be ill

10 What is Alan Jackson's initial reaction when Maria tells him about the aliens she has fought alongside Sarah Jane?

a) He wants to tell Chrissie
b) He argues with Sarah Jane for putting Maria in danger
c) He wants to put the house on the market

ANSWERS: 1.c, 2.b, 3.c, 4.a, 5.a, 6.b, 7.ac, 8.b, 9.b, 10.c.

BRING ON THE BOYS!

Luke was created as part of an alien invasion plan, but now saves Earth on a regular basis alongside his adoptive mum, Sarah Jane. Clyde Langer is the wise-cracking kid who joins the gang when Slitheen take over Park Vale. How well do you know them?

1 Luke was created by the Bane – but they didn't call him Luke. How did Bane villainess Mrs Wormwood refer to him?

a) The Specimen
b) The Experiment
c) The Archetype

2 What kind of sandwiches does Clyde take to school for lunch?

a) Cheese and tomato
b) Cold chip
c) Mashed potato and sausage

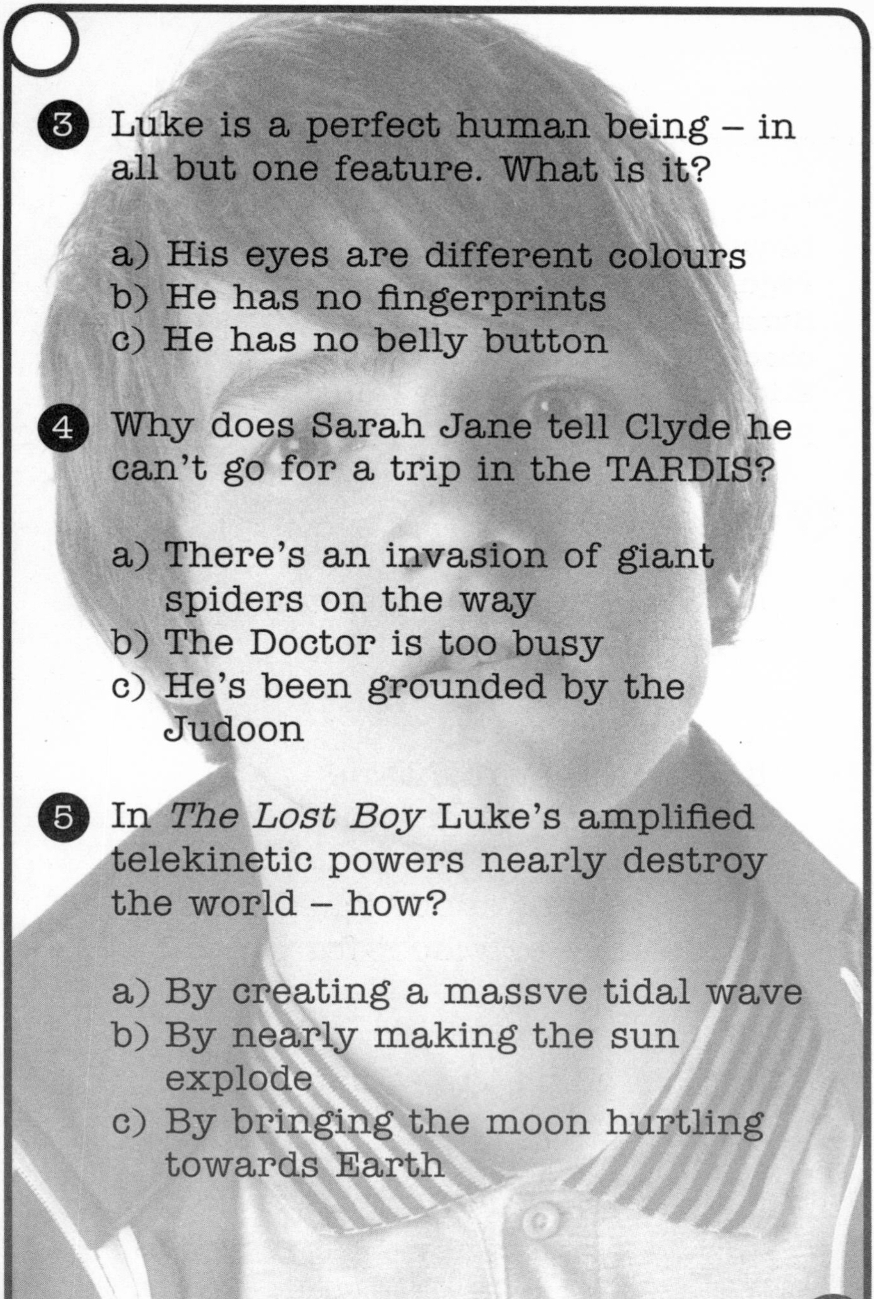

3 Luke is a perfect human being – in all but one feature. What is it?

a) His eyes are different colours
b) He has no fingerprints
c) He has no belly button

4 Why does Sarah Jane tell Clyde he can't go for a trip in the TARDIS?

a) There's an invasion of giant spiders on the way
b) The Doctor is too busy
c) He's been grounded by the Judoon

5 In *The Lost Boy* Luke's amplified telekinetic powers nearly destroy the world – how?

a) By creating a massve tidal wave
b) By nearly making the sun explode
c) By bringing the moon hurtling towards Earth

6 What is Clyde's secret talent?

a) He's a writer
b) He's a singer
c) He's an artist

7 What is it about Luke that enables him to save the population of Earth in *Secrets of the Stars*?

a) His super intelligence.
b) His experience of alien technology
c) His lack of a birth sign

8 Clyde tells Sarah Jane that he has a plan to avoid growing old – what is it?

a) He's never getting married
b) He's going to have his brain put in a robot
c) He's going to become a Time Lord

9 Clyde often refers to Luke as what?

a) His apprentice
b) His minder
c) His Padawan

10 When Mrs Wormwood appears to Luke in a dream in *Enemy of the Bane*, why is he so concerned?

a) She says she's coming to get him
b) He doesn't dream
c) He wasn't asleep

ANSWERS: 1.c, 2.b, 3.c. 4.c, 5.c, 6.c, 7.c, 8.b, 9.c 10.b.

IF YOU GO DOWN TO THE WOODS, THERE'S SOMETHING VERY SCARY WAITING...

Sarah Jane had a shock when Bea Nelson-Stanley mentioned them in *Eye of the Gorgon* – but she's confronted by her oldest enemy of all in *The Last Sontaran*. And Commander Kaagh is a Sontaran with a score to settle. But do you remember how and why?

1. What is the name of the project to which the radio telescope at Goblin's Copse belongs?

   a) Pharos
   b) Tycho
   c) CETI

2. What is the name of Professor Skinner's daughter?

   a) Lucy
   b) Laura
   C) Lisa

3 Which Napoleonic battle does Sarah Jane discover Luke and Clyde recreating with Mr Smith's help?

a) Trafalgar
b) Waterloo
c) Leipzig

4 What star was the radio telescope meant to be observing when it was buzzed by strange lights in the sky?

a) Rigel Beta 5
b) Proxima Centauri
c) Metebilis 3

5 According to Sarah Jane, the Vorkazian Hoards of Meta Vorka 6 travel in a spacecraft the size of what?

a) A small family car
b) A washing machine
c) A coffee cup

6 What does Luke say is responsible for hiding the Sontaran spaceship?

a) A very big bush
b) An invisibility meta-field
c) A perception camouflage matrix

7 Who foiled the Sontarans' plan to invade Earth and destroyed Kaagh's mothership?

a) Sarah Jane
b) Torchwood
c) The Doctor

8 When Sarah Jane is captured and with only forty minutes to save Earth, who does Maria call for help?

a) Mr Smith
b) Alan Jackson
c) Chrissie Jackson

9 What do Clyde and Maria try to remove in order to sabotage the telescope?

a) The tracking guidance system
b) The central control system transponder
c) The swing bearing

10 What does Chrissie use to overcome Commander Kaagh?

a) Her shoe
b) Alan's belt
c) Kaagh's gun

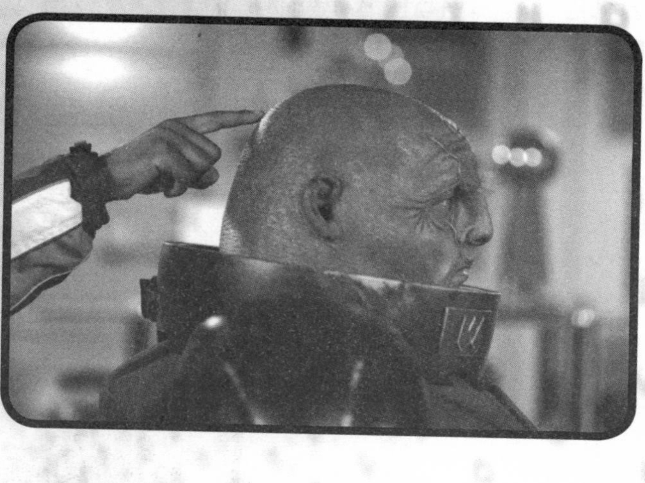

ANSWERS: 1.b, 2.a, 3.b, 4.a, 5.c, 6.c, 7.c, 8.b, 9.b, 10.a.

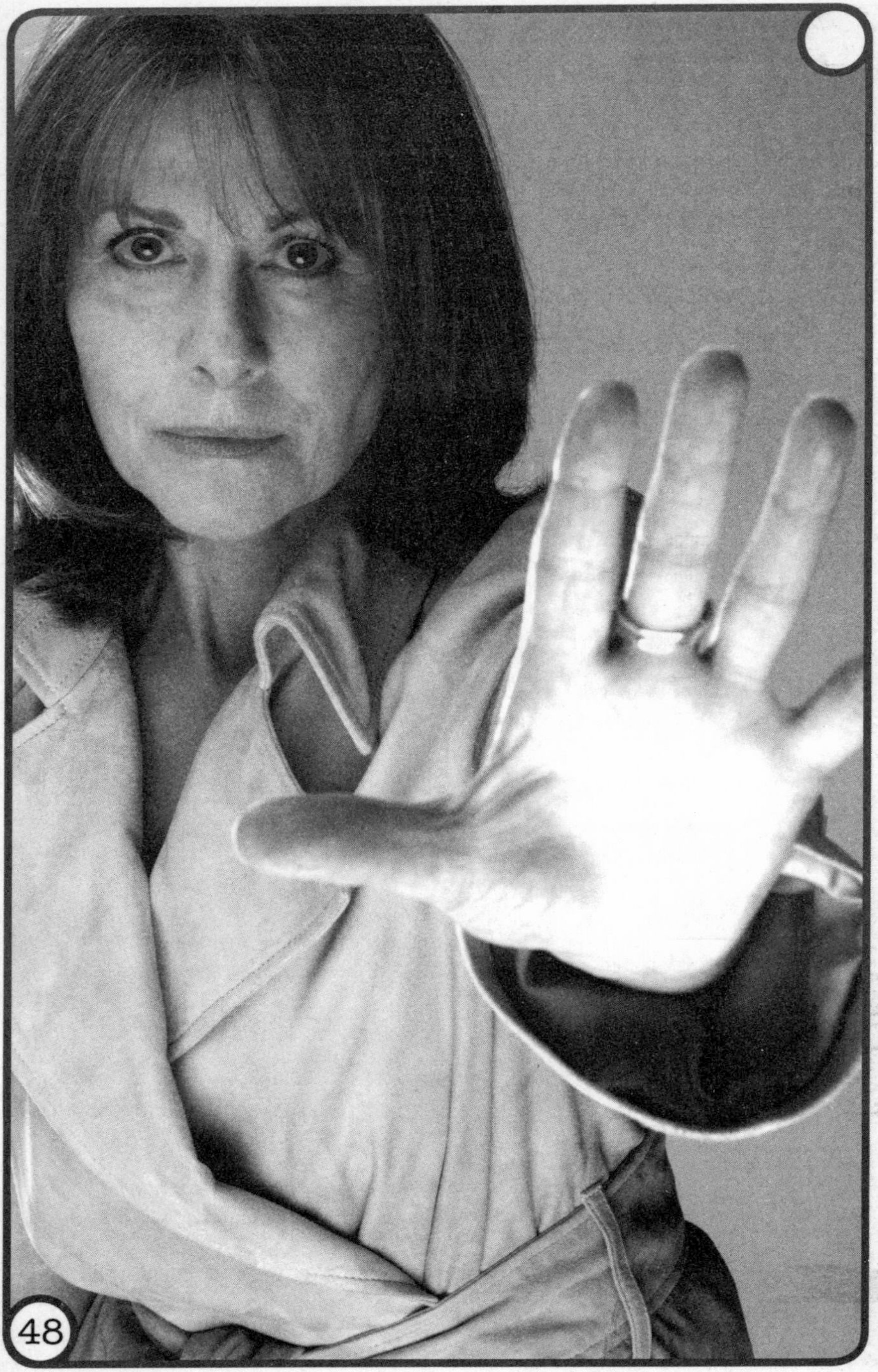

COULD YOU DEFEND THE EARTH FROM THESE UNIVERSAL VILLAINS?

Sarah Jane and her team have taken on plenty of threats from outer space – but, as Clyde says, sometimes it feels like there's a big sign hanging over Earth saying 'PLEASE INVADE', so maybe you've lost track of who is who. Let's find out, shall we?

1. ____________________________________

2. ______________________

3. ______________________

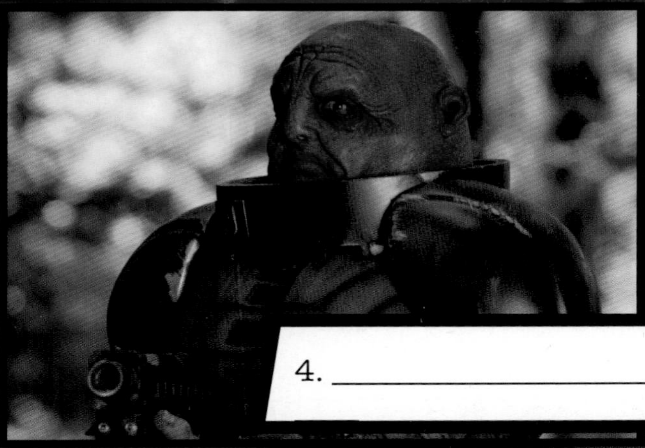

4. ______________________

5. ______________________________

6. ______________________________

7. ______________________________

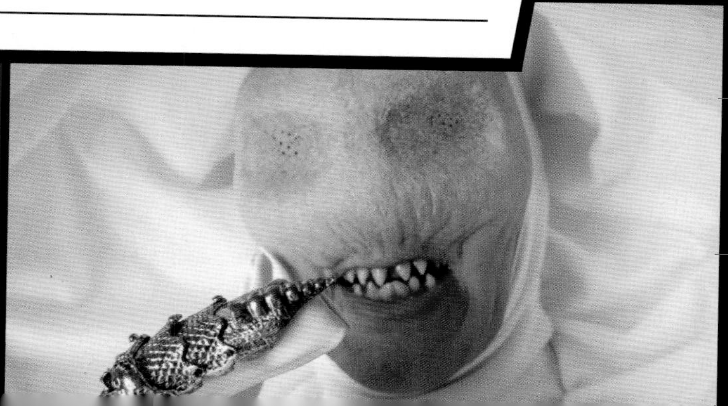

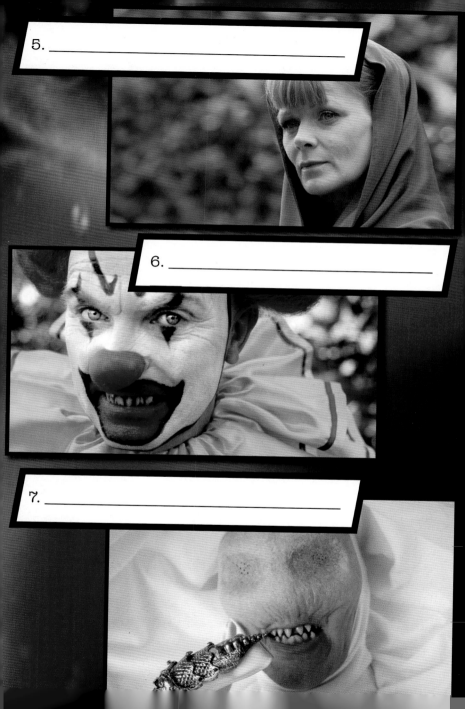

8. ______________________________

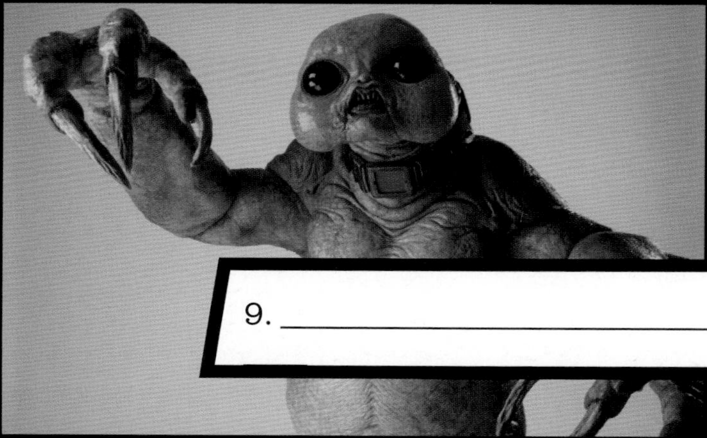

9. ______________________________

10. ______________________________

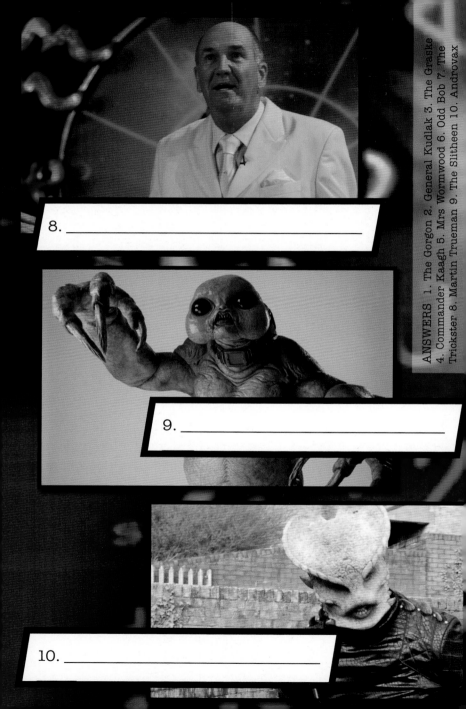

ANSWERS 1. The Gorgon 2. General Kudlak 3. The Graske 4. Commander Kaagh 5. Mrs Wormwood 6. Odd Bob 7. The Trickster 8. Martin Trueman 9. The Slitheen 10. Androvax

RIEND OR FOE?

During their adventures, Sarah Jane and her gang have encountered lots of people – from this world and others – but which of them have been riends, and which have been not so friendly?

1. Cheryl Farley
FRIEND/ FOE?

2. Mrs Wormwood
FRIEND/ FOE?

3. Sister Helena
FRIEND/FOE?
4. Major Kilburne
FRIEND/ FOE?
5. Professor Rivers
FRIEND/ FOE?

6. Harry Sowersby
FRIEND/ FOE?

7. Captain Tybo
FRIEND/ FOE?

8. Nathan Goss
FRIEND/ FOE?

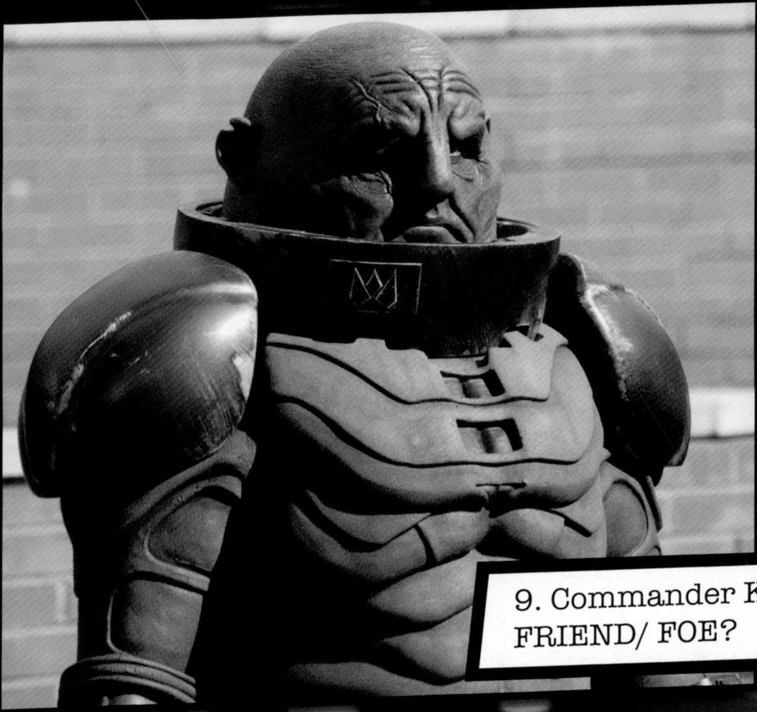

9. Commander Kaagh
FRIEND/ FOE?

10. Brigadier Sir Alistair Gordon Lethbridge-Stewart
FRIEND/ FOE?

ANSWERS 1. Foe, 2. Foe, 3. Foe, 4. Foe, 5. Friend, 6. Friend, 7. Foe, 8. Foe, 9. Foe, 10. Friend.

CAN YOU SURVIVE THE CLIFFHANGER?

Sarah Jane's adventures have been pretty hair-raising at times, and whether it's been taking on Mrs Wormwood and the Bane, the Trickster or Odd Bob the Clown, one thing is always for sure – somewhere along the line there's going to be a nail-biting cliffhanger ending. But are these cliffhangers true or false?

1. Episode one of *Secrets of the Stars* ended with Rani being taken over by the Ancient Lights and preparing to destroy Sarah Jane.

   TRUE/FALSE

2. As episode one of *The Temptation of Sarah Jane* drew to a close, Sarah Jane discovered that saving her parents had led to the devastation of modern day Earth by the Trickster.

   TRUE/FALSE

3 Alan Jackson was turned to stone at the end of the first part of *Eye of the Gorgon.*

TRUE/FALSE

4 Sarah Jane and Rani face being eaten alive by the Bane at the cliffhanger of *Enemy of the Bane*.

TRUE/FALSE

5 Clyde is de-materialised by evil Mr Smith at the end of the first part of *The Lost Boy*.

TRUE/FALSE

6 As episode one of *The Wedding of Sarah Jane Smith* draws to a close The Doctor bursts in to stop the wedding.

TRUE/FALSE

7 The cliffhanger of *Day of the Clown* sees Rani terrorised in her kitchen by Odd Bob the Clown.

TRUE/FALSE

8 Maria finds herself transported to 1964 and meets a very young Sarah Jane Smith at the end of part one of *Whatever Happened to Sarah Jane?*

TRUE/ FALSE

9 Activating Mr Smith at the end of episode one of *Prisoner of the Judoon* starts his self-destruct protocols.

TRUE/FALSE

10 In *Revenge of the Slitheen* Clyde and Maria are cornered by a Slitheen child in the cliffhanger.

TRUE/ FALSE

ANSWERS:
1. False. 2. True. 3. True. 4. False. 5. True.
6. True. 7. False. 8. True. 9. True. 10. True.

SOMETIMES CLOWNS JUST AREN'T A LAUGHING MATTER

When children started going missing from Park Vale, Sarah Jane had something much closer to home on her mind – new neighbours moving in to the house over the road, including a very curious girl called Rani. Do you remember if there was anything to laugh about in *The Day of The Clown?*

1. Who does Luke get an email from just before he hears that they have new neighbours?

   a) Clyde
   b) Maria
   c) Professor Rivers

2. What does Mr Chandra call Clyde when he first meets him in the classroom?

   a) The class clown
   b) The joker in the pack
   c) The Park Vale punster

3. Why does Sarah Jane visit Gita while she's unpacking from the move?

   a) She's looking for alien life
   b) Maria left the puzzle box behind
   c) She wants to warn them about strange things happening

4. With which fairy tale character is Odd Bob associated with?

   a) The Pied Piper
   b) Red Riding Hood
   c) Rumplestiltskin

5. Mr Smith tells Sarah Jane that Odd Bob was responsible for disappearances in America. But when?

   a) 1960-65
   b) 1922-25
   c) 1932-40

6 What helps Sarah Jane and the team escape from Spellman's Magical Museum of the Circus?

a) A fire extinguisher
b) The sonic lipstick
c) Rani's phone

7 How did Odd Bob get to Earth?

a) A spaceship
b) A meteor
c) A beam of light

8 What scared Sarah Jane as a child and gave her a fear of clowns?

a) A Jack-in-the-box
b) A puppet
c) A fairy story

9 What does Spellman use to control the Park Vale kids and bring them to the museum?

a) A flute
b) Ice cream
c) Balloons

10 How does Clyde defeat Spellman?

a) He tells jokes
b) He traps him in a time fissure
c) He corners him in the hall of mirrors

ANSWERS: 1.b, 2.b, 3.a, 4.a, 5.c, 6.c, 7.b, 8.b, 9.c, 10.a.

IT'S ALL IN THE STARS!

Sarah Jane doesn't believe in astrology, but when fake fortune teller Martin Trueman is taken over by a powerful alien intelligence in *Secrets of the Stars*, she and the gang come to realise that for once their fate really is at the mercy of the stars. Will your score be, too?

1 What does Trueman tell his client, Cheryl, will be lost?

a) Some money
b) A letter
c) A ring

2 Which star sign is Clyde?

a) Sagittarius
b) Leo
c) Gemini

3. Who has dropped out of the Psychic Channel's *Paranormal Planet* show?

a) Celestial Deidre
b) Psychic Sam
c) Astrological Stella

4. When Trueman attacks Sarah Jane and Rani, what does Mr Smith tell them has burned a hole in the jacket?

a) A laser beam
b) Sonic energy
c) Nothing

5. Which sign of the zodiac is the first to come under Trueman's control?

a) Gemini
b) Leo
c) Taurus

6 Where do the Ancient Lights come from?

a) Proxima Centauri
b) Saturn
c) Another universe

7 Luke stops Trueman's broadcast to the world by doing what?

a) Turning off the power
b) Smashing the TV camera
c) Locking him in a cupboard

8 In order for the Ancient Lights to take over the world every star in the universe has to be in perfect conjunction for the first time in how many years?

a) 100 years
b) 60,000 years
c) 13 billion years

9 When Trueman is defeated, what happens to him?

a) He joins the Ancient Lights
b) He is arrested
c) He turns into an old man

10 What are Clyde's stars for the day, according to *The Ealing Echo*?

a) You will save the world
b) You will find love in a laundrette
c) You will meet a stranger

ANSWERS: 1.b, 2.c, 3.a, 4.c, 5.a, 6.c, 7.a, 8.c, 9.a, 10.b.

CLYDE QUOTES

Okay, so we all know that Clyde Langer is the coolest kid at Park Vale Comprehensive – at least, as far as Clyde is concerned, he is. And aliens beware – when invading Earth it's not just Sarah Jane you'll have to worry about – there's also the biting Clyde wit. But do you know which episodes featured these sparks of Langer genius?

1 "When weirdo nuns turn up on your doorstep asking about freaky glowing alien gizmos, one thing you never do is tell them you've got one!"

a) *Eye of the Gorgon*
b) *Warriors of Kudlak*
c) *Whatever Happened to Sarah Jane?*

2 "Best part of being in this team? Running away afterwards."

a) *The Last Sontaran*
b) *Enemy of the Bane*
c) *Secrets of the Stars*

3. "I am one of the Inner Circle and know all the mysteries of the stars. Mars has entered the Milky Way and Aero is in conjunction with the Galaxy."

   a) *Enemy of the Bane*
   b) *Secrets of the Stars*
   c) *Revenge of the Slitheen*

4. "We've seen off all sorts of aliens. No way is Earth going down to the Baked Spud From Outer Space!"

   a) *Enemy of the Bane*
   b) *The Last Sontaran*
   c) *Whatever Happened to Sarah Jane?*

5. "It's Attack of the One-Eyed Squiddy Things!"

   a) *Enemy of the Bane*
   b) *The Lost Boy*
   c) *Invasion of the Bane*

6 "From what I've seen, one alien can be as much trouble as a whole invasion."

a) *Warriors of Kudlak*
b) *The Day of the Clown*
c) *Eye of the Gorgon*

7 "Okay I have gone past worried. I'm not even stopping at anxious. I am full throttle into totally panicked beyond reason."

a) *The Last Sontaran*
b) *The Day of The Clown*
c) *Warriors of Kudlak*

8 "I hate the woods. The city is civilisation. This is the Land that Time Forgot."

a) *The Last Sontaran*
b) *Enemy of the Bane*
c) *The Mark of the Berserker*

9 "I wish to serve you. I wish to join the Pantheon."

a) *The Wedding of Sarah Jane Smith*
b) *The Day of the Clown*
c) *The Temptation of Sarah Jane Smith*

10 "Like museums don't normally creep me out – all those stuffed animals, bones and mummies. But this place doesn't just take the biscuit. This place gets the whole Christmas tin."

a) *Revenge of the Slitheen*
b) *The Day of the Clown*
c) *Enemy of the Bane*

ANSWERS: 1.a, 2.c, 3.b, 4.b, 5.a, 6.b, 7.c, 8.a, 9.a, 10.b.

FATHER AND SON

When Clyde's run-away dad shows up on his doorstep it starts to look like father and son have the chance to make up for lost time. Until Clyde's dad gets his hands on an alien pendant with sinister powers. And with Sarah Jane out of town in *The Mark of the Berserker* Luke and Rani have to call for help from an old friend to sort things out. How much do you remember?

1. What is the name of the boy who has the Berserker pendant during school detention?

   a) Steve
   b) Peter
   c) Jacob

2. Sarah Jane tells Clyde's mum, Carla, that she is going away to work on a story about what?

   a) Hospital hygiene
   b) Hospital waiting lists
   c) Hospital patients going missing

3. What does Rani tell her dad she has in her pocket?

   a) Change from buying a pizza
   b) The Berserker pendant
   c) A hamster

4. What is Clyde's dad's name?

   a) Clint
   b) Wes
   c) Paul

5. What does Clyde tell his dad on the swings?

   a) That he has saved the world
   b) That he wants to be an artist
   c) That he hates school

6. What does Haresh start to do whilst talking to Clyde and his dad outside Sarah Jane's house?

   a) Eat a pizza
   b) Exercise
   c) Laugh for no reason

7. Who do Luke and Rani turn to for help when Clyde forgets them and leaves with his dad?

a) Sarah Jane
b) Maria and Alan Jackson
c) Professor Rivers

8. What musical instrument does Clyde's dad give him, after using the pendant to get it?

a) Guitar
b) Saxophone
c) Drum kit

9. Where does Sarah Jane find Clyde and his dad before beating the Berserker?

a) An airport
b) A car park
c) A marina

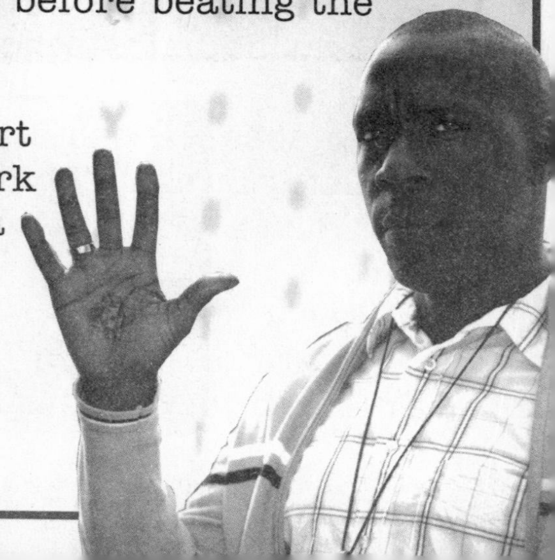

10 Before disposing of the pendant for good, Clyde does what with it?

a) Makes his mum forget about aliens
b) Makes his dad fall in love with his mum again
c) Makes Luke cool

ANSWERS: 1.c, 2.a, 3.c, 4.c, 5.a, 6.b, 7.b, 8.a, 9.c, 10.a.

TRICKY TIME TRAVEL

In *The Temptation of Sarah Jane Smith* an old adversary returned to pit his wits against her in what was to become Sarah Jane's most harrowing adventure ever - and saw her make the most difficult decision of her life. Can you make the right choices now?

1. What is the name of the boy who comes through the time fissure?

   a) Arnold
   b) Bernard
   c) Oscar

2. Sarah Jane goes through the time fissure and finds herself looking at the place she was born – what is its name?

   a) Foxgrove
   b) Foxhill
   c) Foxglade

3 What are Sarah Jane's parents called?

a) Beryl and Eric
b) Betty and Ernie
c) Barbara and Eddie

4 What names do Sarah Jane and Luke use as a cover when they arrive at the fete?

a) Cheryl and Ashley Cole
b) Coleen and Wayne Rooney
c) Victoria and David Beckham

5 How many gobstoppers does Luke correctly estimate are in the jar?

a) 502
b) 676
c) 703

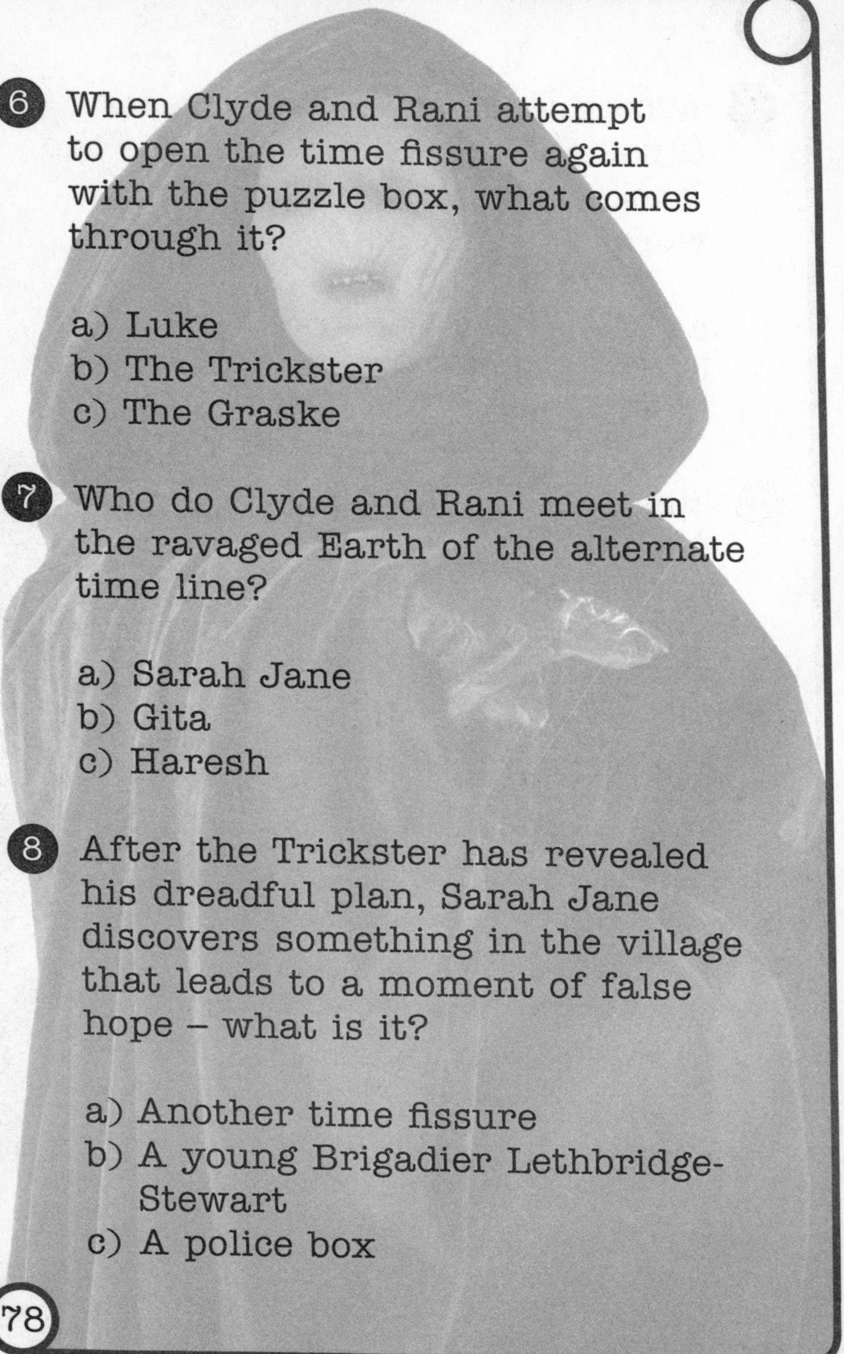

6 When Clyde and Rani attempt to open the time fissure again with the puzzle box, what comes through it?

a) Luke
b) The Trickster
c) The Graske

7 Who do Clyde and Rani meet in the ravaged Earth of the alternate time line?

a) Sarah Jane
b) Gita
c) Haresh

8 After the Trickster has revealed his dreadful plan, Sarah Jane discovers something in the village that leads to a moment of false hope – what is it?

a) Another time fissure
b) A young Brigadier Lethbridge-Stewart
c) A police box

9 According to the legend that Clyde and Rani hear, what did the Trickster walk through into the world?

a) The Priest's Arch
b) The Abbot's Gate
c) The Vicar's Doorway

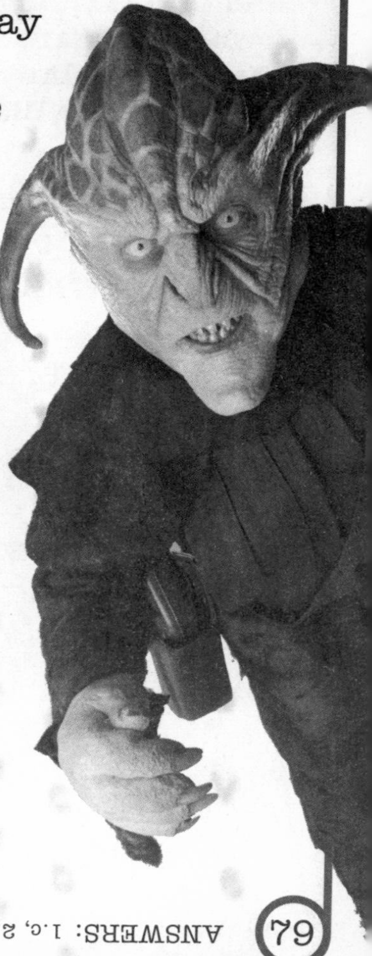

10 What does Clyde give to the Graske in return for his help?

a) The puzzle box
b) His mobile phone
c) His mp3 player

ANSWERS: 1.c, 2.a, 3.c, 4.c, 5.b, 6.c, 7.b, 8.c, 9.b, 10.a.

BE CAREFUL OF YOUR ENEMIES – THEY MIGHT EAT YOU!

Sarah Jane finds herself entering into a very uneasy alliance in *Enemy of the Bane* and also looking up an old friend as people and things from the past come back to haunt both Sarah Jane and Luke – and threaten the whole galaxy. Do you remember all the secrets of the Black Archive?

1. When Gita is kidnapped from the flower shop, Luke finds a clue there to her abductor – but what is it?

   a) A fingerprint
   b) A cheque
   c) A note

2. Where does Mrs Wormwood tell Sarah Jane they should have launched Bubbleshock?

   a) America
   b) Japan
   c) Australia

3 What does Mrs Wormwood tell Sarah Jane the Bane do to those who fail them?

a) Eat them alive
b) Exile them to a barren moon
c) Cast them adrift in space

4 Who ruled the Dark Empire?

a) Clyde's dad
b) Vlad the Impaler
c) Horath

5 What is hidden in the Black Archive?

a) The Eye of the Gorgon
b) The Tunguska Scroll
c) The Berserker Pendant

6 To whom does Sarah Jane turn in order to enter the Black Archive?

a) Mrs Wormwood
b) Brigadier Sir Alistair Lethbridge-Stewart
c) Major Kilburne

7. Who saves Mrs Wormwood from the Bane in Sarah Jane's garden?

   a) Sarah Jane
   b) Kaagh
   c) Brigadier Sir Alistair Lethbridge-Stewart

8. Where do Sarah Jane and the gang hide from UNIT?

   a) The attic
   b) Gita's flower shop
   c) Park Vale School

9. Who does Gita find at Sarah Jane's house and take home for tea?

   a) Commander Kaagh
   b) Brigadier Sir Alistair Lethbridge-Stewart
   c) Major Kilburne

10 At what kind of ancient site is Horath supposedly hidden?

a) A church cemetery
b) A circle of standing stones
c) A castle

ANSWERS: 1.b, 2.a, 3.a, 4.c, 5.b, 6.b, 7.b, 8.b, 9.c, 10.b.

JUMPIN' JUDOON!

When a Judoon ship crashes, Sarah Jane gets more than she bargained for with a villain who hides in the strangest of places. Do you think you could track down the *Prisoner of the Judoon*? Let's see...

1 What is the name of the laboratories where Sarah Jane meets Mr Yorke?

a) Genius
b) Giant
c) Genetec

2 Where does Mr Smith tell the gang that Captain Tybo's ship has crashed?

a) The Brindley Chase Estate
b) The Byrkley Course Estate
c) Buckingham Palace Estate

3 What is the name of Captain Tybo's prisoner?

a) Androvax
b) Alurox
c) Activax

4 Sarah Jane tells the gang that Earth is barely recognised by the Shadow Proclamation – why?

a) It is too far away
b) It is too small
c) It is too primitive

5 How many galaxies is Androvax wanted in for his crimes?

a) Ten
b) Nine
c) Twelve

6 Why does Tybo say he won't turn on the police car's siren and lights?

a) The siren is too loud
b) He's under cover
c) They are broken

7 What does Sarah Jane want the nanoforms to build for her?

a) A space ship
b) A bomb
c) A new house

8 Apart from the gang, who else gets trapped in the laboratory building?

a) A school party
b) The cleaners
c) Haresh and Gita

9 What do Clyde and Rani use to stop the nanoforms when trapped in the lab?

a) Ultra-sonic signal
b) Fire extinguishers
c) A laser

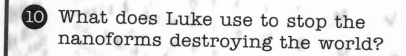

10 What does Luke use to stop the nanoforms destroying the world?

a) The sonic lipstick
b) An alien computer
c) Fire extinguishers

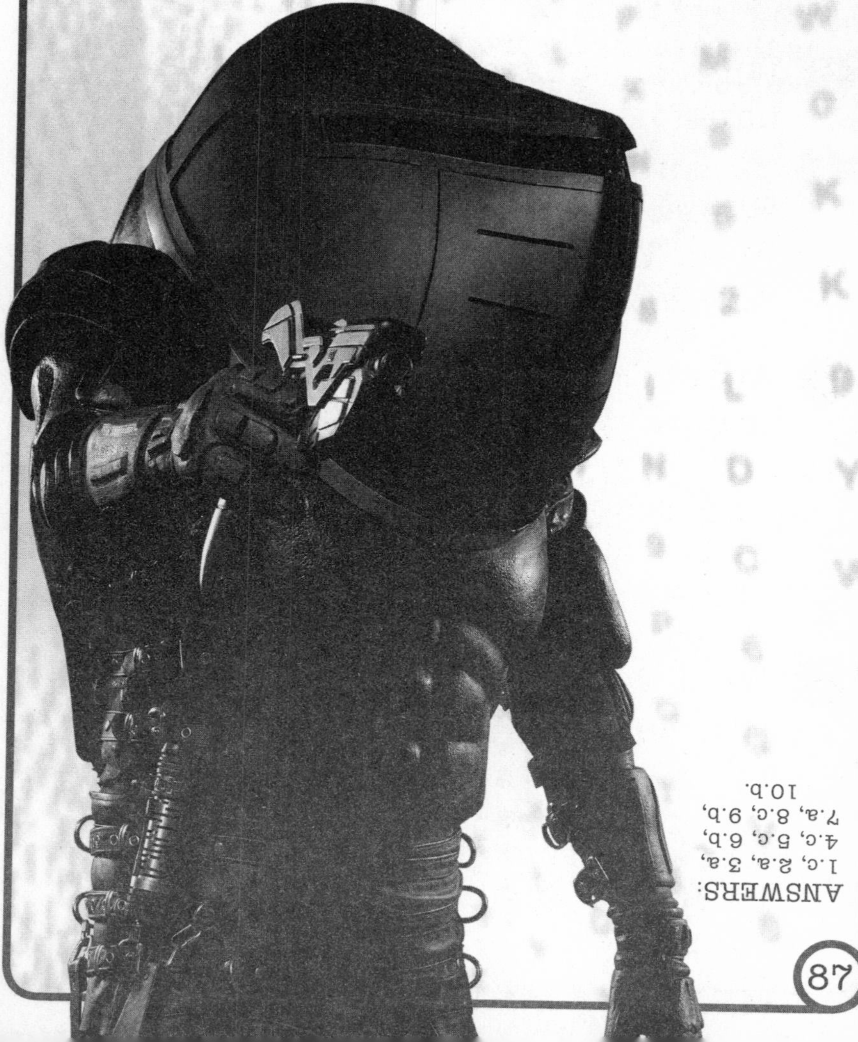

ANSWERS:
1.c, 2.a, 3.a,
4.c, 5.c, 6.b,
7.a, 8.c, 9.b,
10.b.

VILLAINOUS QUOTES

During her adventures Sarah Jane has encountered some pretty fearsome villains – some of them with a line in chat as sharp as their plans for world destruction. But can you remember who said what?

1 "I can feel this moment reverberating back through the ages. The meeting of the Pantheon of Discord and the last of the Time Lords."

a) The Graske
b) Odd Bob
c) The Trickster

2 "She's human. She smelled soupy, they all do."

a) General Kudlak
b) Mr Blakeman
c) Davey the Bane

3 "My name will live for all eternities to come. My people will scream it as a battle-cry."

a) Commander Kaagh
b) General Kudlak
c) Major Kilburne

4 "Today I will chill the blood of a nation. A thousand families will ache with loss, and millions will shudder, sleepless, with a bone-gnawing fear."

a) The Trickster
b) Mrs Wormwood
c) Elijah Spellman

5 "The sweetest delicacy is the tongue of an enemy that has looked at you, and licked their lips."

a) Commander Kaagh
b) Martin Trueman
c) Mrs Wormwood

6 “I’d shut up if I were you, or the Abbess might show you her idea of solving a problem like Maria.”

a) Sister Helena
b) Mrs Wormwood
c) Odd Bob

7 “I was born at exactly the right moment, at exactly the right time. I am the most important person on the planet – on any planet. People used to say, ‘you’re not the centre of the universe’. It turns out I am!”

a) Martin Trueman
b) Sister Helena
c) Paul Langer

8 “Suppose there isn’t anything to be understood. Suppose I am beyond understanding. Suppose, when the thunder crashed and the lightning flashed, your aunt’s clown really did come to life.”

a) Martin Trueman

b) Odd Bob
c) The Trickster

9 "Chaos is my blood and air and food... The meteor is pure chaos – the destruction of Earth for no reason at all. Just blind chance. This is food for me."

a) Odd Bob
b) The Trickster
c) General Kudlak

10 "We all have a purpose. Yours is to die so that the Xylok will live. After all, what life do you have, alone in your attic?"

a) Mrs Wormwood
b) Mr Blakeman
c) Mr Smith

ANSWERS:
1.c, 2.b, 3.a,
4.c, 5.c. 6.a.
7.a. 8.b, 9.b,
10.c.

ALL THE FRIGHT OF THE FAIR!

When Rani decides to investigate a spooky funfair on her own she's headed for real trouble – enough to last a lifetime. So do you remember how things went so wrong for her in *The Mad Woman in the Attic?*

1. Where is the funfair that Rani goes to investigate?

   a) Danemouth
   b) Rhyl
   c) Brighton

2. What is the name of the caretaker that she finds at the funfair?

   a) Arnold
   b) Herbert
   c) Harry

3. How many people is Rani told have gone missing recently?

   a) Four
   b) Five
   c) Six

4. Clyde is prepared to climb over the gates of the funfair – but what does Sarah Jane think is more stylish?

a) Ringing the bell
b) Calling for help
c) Using the sonic lipstick

5. Where do Sarah Jane, Luke and Clyde meet Rani's friend?

a) The funfair
b) A café
c) A children's home

6. How does Ship communicate with the caretaker and later with Sarah Jane?

a) By telephone
b) Through a mirror
c) Through a television

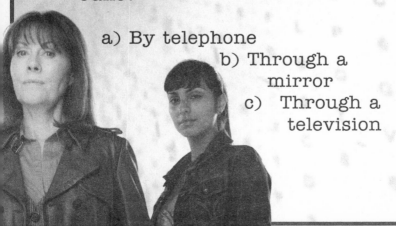

7 Where is Eve's spaceship hidden?

a) Under the beach
b) As part of a funfair ride
c) In the sea

8 When she's been shown her future, what does a dazed Sarah Jane tell Clyde she's seen in that attic?

a) A Dalek
b) The Trickster
c) The TARDIS and the Doctor

9 What does Eve's ship need to fuel it?

a) A black hole
b) A gigantic diamond
c) A lightning strike

10 Who does Rani discover is Adam's mother?

a) Eve
b) Mrs Wormwood
c) Gita

ANSWERS: 1.a, 2.c, 3.a, 4.c, 5.c, 6.b, 7.a, 8.c, 9.a, 10.a.

GUESS WHO'S COMING TO THE WEDDING?

It's the biggest day of Sarah Jane's life – she's going to get married. But Clyde is suspicious and there's going to be a very special surprise guest – can you guess who?

1. The gang follows Sarah Jane because she's been behaving strangely – where has she told them she was going?

   a) The town hall
   b) The library
   c) The theatre

2. Who tells Sarah Jane that Luke, Rani and Clyde have been spying on her?

   a) Haresh and Gita
   b) Mr Smith and K-9
   c) Clyde

3. An alien creature, Travis Polong, arrives in a surprising way – how?

a) It beams down
b) It drives up in a car
c) It comes by post

4. Sarah Jane is going to marry Peter. What is his job?

a) Lawyer
b) Architect
c) Physicist

5. What is different about the Trickster when he first appears at the wedding?

a) He has a face
b) He's a miniature version on the wedding cake
c) He's dressed in white

6 What does the Doctor admit to being on a good day?

a) Pretty amazing
b) Pretty quick
c) Pretty attractive

7 The Trickster traps the Doctor, Luke, Rani, Clyde and K-9 in time – what time, exactly?

a) 3.23.23
b) 5.32.32
c) 6.30.31

8 Why is the TARDIS having difficulty materialising, according to K-9?

a) It's low on fuel
b) Fluctuations in the time flow
c) A temporal schism

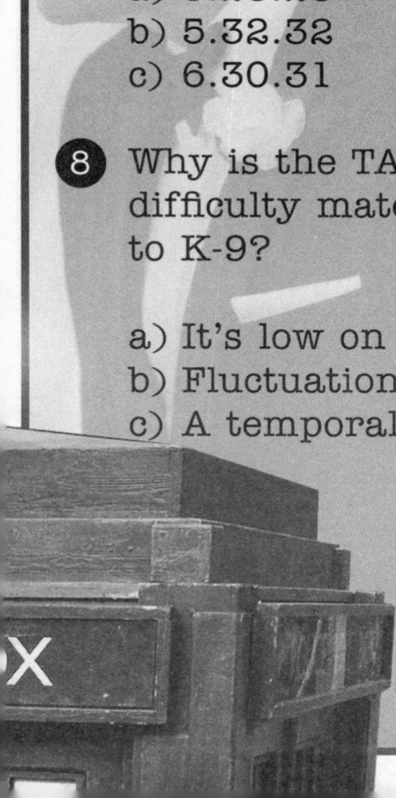

9 What does the Doctor use to silence Luke, Rani and Clyde when they have too many questions to ask?

a) A whistle
b) A football rattle
c) A car horn

10 What sort of energy does Clyde use to try to defeat the Trickster?

a) Chronon Energy
b) Kinetic Energy
c) Artron Energy

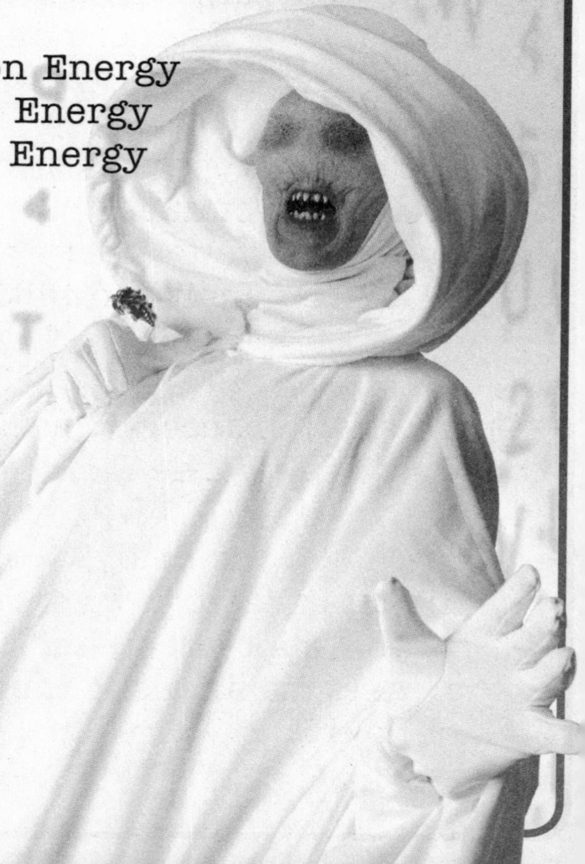

ANSWERS:
1.a, 2.b, 3.c,
4.a, 5.c, 6.a,
7.a, 8.c, 9.b,
10.c.

HAVE YOU GOT WHAT IT TAKES TO JOIN THE GANG IN THE ATTIC?

Sarah Jane doesn't let just anyone into the attic. It takes some special qualities to help her deal with the aliens that visit Earth – friendly, and not so friendly. So now let's see if you've got what it takes to make it as part of the team!

1. There's a giant meteor headed straight for Bannerman Road. Do you...

   a) Run for the nearest disused nuclear bunker?
   b) Get out your trusty catapult?
   c) Ask Mr Smith to initiate a deflection field?

2. An alien spacecraft crashes into your back garden. Do you...

   a) Call in the army?
   b) Start digging, cover it with earth and hope no one notices?
   c) Ask the aliens if they need any help?

3 You wake up one morning and time starts unravelling around you. Do you...

a) Turn over in bed and go back to sleep?
b) Check to make sure there's no one new living over the road?
c) Re-set your watch.

4 Your schoolfriends are mysteriously starting to disappear. Do you...

a) Take on their paper rounds?
b) Make a move on their boy/girl friends?
c) Look out for sudden storms, and make sure you've got an umbrella?